BETH MOORE

so long, *insecurity*

teen edition

Tyndale House Publishers, Inc.

Carol Stream, Illinois

Visit Tyndale online at www.tyndale.com.

Visit Living Proof's website at www.LProof.org.

TYNDALE and Tyndale's quill logo are registered trademarks of Tyndale House Publishers, Inc.

So Long, Insecurity Teen Edition

Designed by Jacqueline L. Nuñez

Published in association with Yates & Yates (www.yates2.com).

Unless otherwise indicated, all Scripture quotations are taken from the *Holy Bible*, New Living Translation, copyright © 1996, 2004, 2007 by Tyndale House Foundation. Used by permission of Tyndale House Publishers, Inc., Carol Stream, Illinois 60188. All rights reserved.

Scripture quotations marked NIV are taken from the Holy Bible, *New International Version,*® NIV.® Copyright © 1973, 1978, 1984, 2011 by Biblica, Inc.™ Used by permission of Zondervan. All rights reserved worldwide. www.zondervan.com.

The names of girls in the interview sections have been changed to protect their privacy.

Library of Congress Cataloging-in-Publication Data

Moore, Beth, date.
    So long, insecurity teen edition / Beth Moore.
        pages cm
    ISBN 978-1-4143-8043-8 (pbk.)
    1. Teenage girls--Religious life. 2. Christian teenagers--Religious life. 3. Security (Psychology)--Religious aspects--Christianity. I. Title.
    BV4551.3.M66 2013
    248.8'33--dc23
                                2012047663

Printed in China

19	18	17	16	15	14	13
7	6	5	4	3	2	1

Contents

Am I Good Enough?

You've probably heard the term *insecurity* tossed around at school or at home. "She's just saying that because she's insecure." "She's insecure about the way she looks." But what does it really mean to be insecure?

Basically, I think insecurity means that you're just not sure of who you are or what you're worth. You think other girls are smarter, prettier, and funnier than you. And deep down, you even wonder if they're more valuable than you. You second-guess yourself all the time, and sometimes you don't even get in the game of life because you just don't think you're good enough. You don't think you are enough!

Insecurity makes you compare yourself to other girls. You say to yourself, *Why can't my hair look like hers? I'd be happy if I got good grades like she does. Why can't I be as popular as that girl? No guy will ever think I'm as beautiful as she is. I just don't measure up. I am not enough.*

If you've ever said or thought any of these things, this book is just for you. We're going to take a close look at the ways insecurity affects us. But best of all, we're going to find out how to wipe out insecurity and learn to live as healthy, secure girls. So come along with me as we begin this adventure together.

fashion
Chapter 1

Q & A with Beth

fashion

what your clothes say about you

Q: Does it really matter what I wear?

A: Let me tell you about two twentysomething women I saw at a restaurant while out with my family one evening. I came face-to-face with just how fierce insecurity can be when it comes to fashion and how we dress. The women both wore very short skirts and low-cut tops, and let's just say they were really making good use out of those push-up bras.

They might have just been trying to be in style and look good, but they were making a statement about how they saw themselves. They thought the only way to get attention was to wear a sign that said, "I'm totally available. Check me out. Look at me." When you dress like that, advertising lots of skin, you are screaming volumes about how you feel inside. You're giving the message that the only thing that makes you valuable as a woman is your body.

But don't we have so much more to offer than our bodies and too much skin? And when it comes down to it, do we really want to attract people who would want us to expose too much of ourselves just to get their attention?

Let me tell you, males know when you are using your clothes (or lack there-of) to get their attention. They are aware it's a sign of insecurity and desperation, and if you're not careful, some guys will take advantage of insecure girls . . . be-cause they know they can. One guy told me, "The more skin girls show, the more insecure they are."

Now, some of you may not be into short skirts or letting your cleavage show. When I was your age, my body was slow in developing, and I was more embarrassed by it than anything. But this idea that what we wear makes a statement about us can apply to other things too. Maybe you wear tons of makeup to try to hide who you really are. Maybe you wear wild clothes or hairstyles just to be different and get attention. Maybe you are obsessed with having the latest trends so people will think you're cool. Maybe you think getting certain piercings or

think about it

❝Don't be concerned about the outward beauty of fancy hairstyles, expensive jewelry, or beautiful clothes. You should clothe yourselves instead with the beauty that comes from within, the unfading beauty of a gentle and quiet spirit, which is so precious to God❞ (1 Peter 3:3-4).

tattoos will put you in the crowd you want to be in.

Insecurity can make you focus too much on having just the right labels, the "in" designer brand. Do you think you'll feel better about yourself only if you have the hottest new items? Do you resent having to shop for clothes at discount stores or resale shops? If so, it's time to check yourself and your insecurity level. If you find that your worth comes from your outward appearance, it's time to find out what God thinks about you.

Let me be clear: I don't think it's wrong to look your best. The problem comes when you're overly focused on your outward appearance—whether that's showing too much skin to get attention or using your clothes to be someone you're not. The thing is, fashion should be fun! Fashion should be about finding your own personal style, not about compromising who you are on the inside.

I think that's why the Bible says,

"Don't be concerned about the outward beauty of fancy hairstyles, expensive jewelry, or beautiful clothes. You should clothe yourselves instead with the beauty that comes from within, the unfading beauty of a gentle and quiet spirit, which is so precious to God" (1 Peter 3:3-4).

You are precious to God because of who you are . . . not because of what you wear or how you look! So let your unfading beauty show from the inside out. Let your inner being shine much more beautifully than your clothes, makeup, and hair. Why? Because you're worth more than what you wear!

wear it well

Being modest doesn't mean that you can't have your own sense of fashion or that you have to dress like your grandma. Check out some of these styles with tips on wearing them well.

problem area

problem area

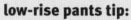

crop-top tip:
wear a tank underneath in a fun, contrasting color ▼

low-rise pants tip:
layer longer shirts; try mixing colors or lace on the bottom ▼

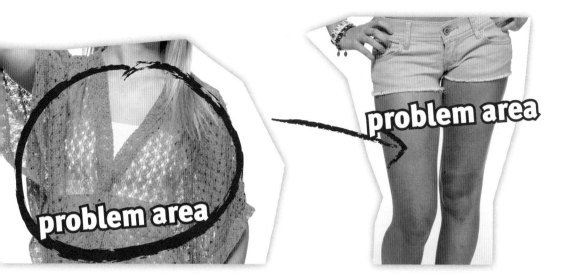

problem area

problem area

open-weave top tip:
wear a tank or cami underneath in a different color ▼

shorts tip:
go a little longer; try a cuff at the bottom ▼

according to God's fashion sense, the way you look on the inside is much more important than the way you dress.

That is why I tell you not to worry about everyday life—whether you have enough food and drink, or enough clothes to wear. Isn't life more than food, and your body more than clothing? Look at the birds. They don't plant or harvest or store food in barns, for your heavenly Father feeds them. And aren't you far more valuable to him than they are? Matthew 6:25-26

She is clothed with strength and dignity; she can laugh at the days to come. *Proverbs 31:25, NIV*

Don't be concerned about the outward beauty of fancy hairstyles, expensive jewelry, or beautiful clothes. You should clothe yourselves instead with the beauty that comes from within, the unfading beauty of a gentle and quiet spirit, which is so precious to God.
1 Peter 3:3-4

We are God's masterpiece. He has created us anew in Christ Jesus, so we can do the good things he planned for us long ago.
Ephesians 2:10

THE LORD SAID TO SAMUEL, "DON'T JUDGE BY HIS APPEARANCE OR HEIGHT, FOR I HAVE REJECTED HIM. THE LORD DOESN'T SEE THINGS THE WAY YOU SEE THEM. PEOPLE JUDGE BY OUTWARD APPEARANCE, BUT THE LORD LOOKS AT THE HEART." I SAMUEL 16:7

Your Stats

15% SAY ○
Magazines

6% SAY ○
Siblings

where do you get your ideas on

clothes/fashion?

54% SAY ○
Friends

18% SAY ○
"I set my
own trends"

7% SAY ○
Store Model

Interviews with Real Girls

what gives you confidence?

I get confidence from reading Scripture and reminding myself of God's plan for me.
— Hannah

I know that God created me to be who I am and that He loves me no matter what. That gives me confidence.
— Madison

how do you build confidence on difficult days?

When I need some encouragement, I talk to someone who cares about me. It gives me confidence to know I am loved.
— Chelsea

I BUILD CONFIDENCE THROUGH THE LOVE AND SECURITY OF MY FAMILY AND FRIENDS, AND THE NEVER-FAILING KNOWLEDGE THAT GOD LOVES ME FOR ME.
— ALYSSA

When I'm feeling down, I remember that God has given me what I need to get through.
— Stephanie

What's Your Style?

got it?
take this quiz to see what your clothes say about you.

Circle the answer that best fits you.

1. **When you select your clothes, you**
a. dress as much like the popular crowd as possible.
b. stop and ask yourself why you want to wear what you've chosen. If your motives are cool, you go with it.
c. wear what you think would impress the cute guy in your social studies class.

2. **You normally wear clothes that are**
a. too tight.
b. just the right size.
c. a few sizes too large so you can hide behind your clothes.

3. **When you go shopping, you**
a. go straight to the trendiest place. You wouldn't be caught dead in an off brand.
b. stop at any place that has clothes you think are cute.
c. buy whatever your mom tells you to get.

4. **Which phrase describes your fashion sense?**

a. Just like a fashion magazine
b. Uniquely mine
c. Who cares about fashion?

5. **When you see a model showing too much skin in an ad, you tend to think,**
a. *Oh, I'd wear that if I had a body like hers.*
b. *Maybe if I wore a tank top under it, it would be cute and wouldn't show too much skin.*
c. *I wouldn't wear that if you paid me.*

If you have mostly *a*'s: Girlfriend, reread this chapter. Check your motives about the way you dress, and take some time to think about what statement your clothes are making about you.
If you have mostly *b*'s: You set your own style. Go, girl! Keep striving to let your confidence and your true beauty shine through.
If you have mostly *c*'s: Fashion might not be your thing, and that's okay. Just make sure you're being true to yourself.

Bible Girl

Esther: MORE THAN A BEAUTY QUEEN

Read Esther 2–9.

MY STATUS: I was a Jewish girl, and my parents died when I was young. After I became an orphan, my relative Mordecai took care of me.

BIG BREAK: When Mordecai and I were living in Persia, the king was looking for a new queen. The king's advisers selected several beautiful girls to try out for queen— kind of like a beauty contest. I was chosen as one of the finalists. I went through a full year of beauty treatments, just to be in the contest. And to my surprise, I won! I became Queen Esther.

THE PROBLEM: My story doesn't end there, however. Mordecai found out that the king's right-hand man didn't like Jews. In fact, he had come up with a plan to kill all the Jews in Persia. Mordecai told me what was going on, and he asked me to talk to the king so I could help our people.

This was a really big deal though. You see, even though I was queen, I couldn't just go up and talk to the king anytime I wanted to. I could have been killed for approaching him without a special appointment. It would have been a lot easier to ignore the problem and sit back and enjoy being queen. But I knew I needed to do what was right—I needed to help my people. But it was going to take a lot of courage.

With God's help, I carefully approached the king. He agreed to change the plan, and in the end, the guy who hated the Jews was the one who was killed. My people were saved!

Chat about It

Gather a group of girls and discuss these questions together.

1. Esther's life shows that we're created for more than just look- ing beautiful. What might have happened if Esther had just seen herself as a beauty queen, not a helper for her people?

2. How would you describe your fashion style? What statement do your clothes make about you?

3. In 1 Peter 3:3-4, the Bible talks about "the beauty that comes from within." What do you think that means? Can you think of someone who has that kind of beauty?

4. Are there some clothes in your closet you need to get rid of or clothes you need to rethink the way you wear them? Grab a friend and do it now!

Dear Jesus,

YOU ARE MY
ONE
TRUE
LOVE
MY ONLY
LOVE

Love always,
Me

media hype
Chapter 2

Q & A with Beth

what does real beauty look like?

Q: I watch movies and go online, but I don't think it affects me that much. Is it really that big of a deal?

A: That's a great question! I think media—TV, movies, magazines, ads, social media, and the stuff we see online—can all play a role in making us insecure. But it doesn't have to be that way! We may not be able to completely stop those media images from bombarding us, but we do have a choice in how much we listen to those messages.

In a lot of ways, I think your generation has it harder than your mom's or your grandmother's generation. Believe it or not, there was a time when we had only about five or six channels to choose from. There was a time when cable TV didn't exist and the Internet hadn't been invented yet. Back when I was a girl, TV programs went off at midnight or so. We used to see color bars on the screen if we were up

late and had the TV on. We didn't have computers or the Internet. Our phones were attached to the wall, not things we could carry with us in our pockets. We'd never heard of texting, and we didn't know what a smartphone was.

But now you can watch TV 24-7—and you can watch any type of program whenever you want. There are networks dedicated to music videos, sports, movies, animals, cartoons, sci-fi (and we still can't find anything to watch! Go figure!). And with the invention of smartphones, tablets, and other gadgets, you can take in media at school, on the bus, at a coffee shop, in bed . . . anywhere!

Think about it: we get flooded with media images practically all day long, and what kinds of women are featured on-screen? They're all seemingly perfect—unrealistically thin and beautiful—and they set an impossible standard for women today. What we don't see is what happens behind the scenes—that these models and actresses have people doing their makeup and hair, and that in many cases their images are manipulated on a computer before you ever see them.

How can you feel good about yourself when you're constantly looking at women who have perfect hair, perfect makeup, a gym body, and the latest clothes? I once read an article that said, "Women who are surrounded by other attractive women, whether in the flesh, in films, or in photographs, rate themselves as less satisfied with their attractiveness." That means that the more pretty girls we see in the media, the less attractive we become in our own eyes. And with so many "perfect" women being paraded all over TV, ads, movie screens, and the Internet, we're faced with a tough challenge every day.

I wish we could use media to turn this around—to help people recognize that beauty comes in many different shapes, sizes, ethnicities, heights, hair colors, and body types. But unfortunately the media gives us a really limited definition of what beautiful looks like. Whether we strive to live up to that ideal or not, it's easy to start feeling insecure about ourselves. It's easy to forget the way our Creator sees us.

What would happen if . . .

. . . we really believed that God created us in His own image?

. . . we really accepted that God sees us, His creation, as very good?

. . . we really saw ourselves as children of God, created to be like Jesus and to live out God's purpose for us?

If we really believed all that . . .

. . . could we really hate our body parts and say things like, "I wish my hair were straighter!" "I wish my hair were curlier!" "I wish my hair were thicker!"?

. . . could we really say, "I'm too skinny!" "I'm too fat!" "I have the wrong shape!"?

. . . could we really say, "My nose is too big!" "My ears are too big!" "My eyes are too small!"?

I'm not saying we have to walk around thinking we look perfect. I just think we should put the negativity in check and stop comparing ourselves to other people. Our whole outlook changes when we start viewing ourselves from God's perspective. After all, He didn't create us to look like someone else. He created each of us just right, the way we are.

And God didn't stop when He created our bodies. He also gave us unique minds, personalities, and souls—things that matter even more than outward appearance. And you can't see someone's personality or mind from a picture or a movie, no matter how hard you try. Don't let someone's beautiful face or seemingly perfect body fool you into thinking you're somehow not good enough the way you are. Let your beauty shine from the inside.

There's no way around it—the media can make us insecure. But we have a much more reliable source to show us what's true: God's Word. We can rest in the security of knowing how our Creator sees us. He created us in His image, which means we have unspeakable value. He created each of us to live a life of purpose—in a way that uses our unique gifts to bring Him glory. And most of all, God created us to live in a right relationship with Him through Christ (see Romans 5:17-19). God created us to be beautiful from the inside out!

behind the scenes

When we see photos of women in ads, most of us have no idea that these images aren't reality. Here's a glimpse into what happens behind the scenes.

There's a reason you never see a model having a bad hair day. Many use extensions, hairpieces, and even wigs to get that full-bodied, picture-perfect look. And on top of that, models have their hair styled by professionals right before they go on the set or get their photo taken.

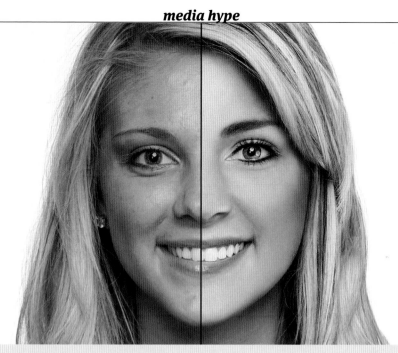

Thanks to technology, there are now more tools than ever to make things look different than they appear in real life. With the click of a mouse, a skin blemish can disappear, hair color can be changed, and a stomach can magically become flat. No wonder we feel like we can't measure up!

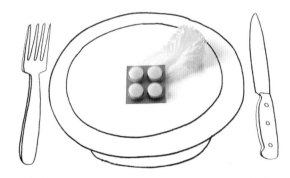

Some women in the camera's view go to dangerous extremes to keep the superslim look. They might take harmful pills or go on unhealthy fad diets, or they might work out excessively. In putting such an unbalanced emphasis on their weight, they can end up causing permanent damage to the bodies God gave them.

Some models and stars have surgery to get the perfect face, nose, or body. These surgeries can be painful, dangerous, and expensive, not to mention that they ignore the natural beauty given to them by their Creator.

God created you, and He is pleased with His handiwork. live like God's special creation!

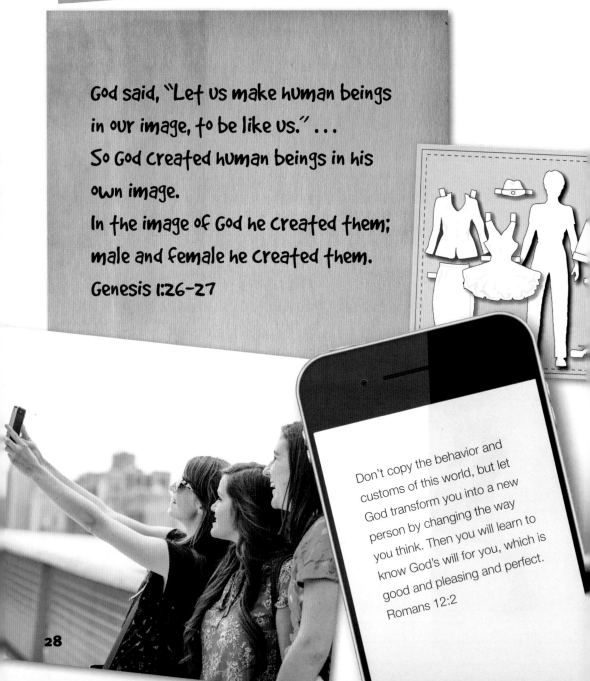

God said, "Let us make human beings in our image, to be like us." . . .
So God created human beings in his own image.
In the image of God he created them; male and female he created them.
Genesis 1:26–27

Don't copy the behavior and customs of this world, but let God transform you into a new person by changing the way you think. Then you will learn to know God's will for you, which is good and pleasing and perfect.
Romans 12:2

Should the thing that was created say to the one who created it, "Why have you made me like this?"
Romans 9:20

God looked over all he had made, and he saw that it was very good! Genesis 1:31

Like · Comment · Share

Chat (5)

how much time do you spend using

social media

in an average week?

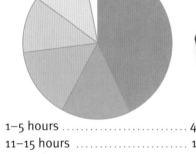

1–5 hours 43%
11–15 hours 15%
16–20 hours 15%
More than 20 hours per week 12%
6–10 hours......................... 12%
Less than 1 hour.................... 3%

how much time do you spend

watching tv

in an average week?

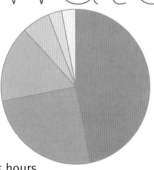

1–5 hours 47%
6–10 hours......................... 25%
11–15 hours........................ 16%
16–20 hours 6%
21–25 hours 3%
None 3%

Interviews with Real Girls

how do images in the media affect the way you feel about yourself?

Seeing the images makes me feel very in-secure even though I know they are fake.

—Sarah

When I see all the pictures of famous people looking flaw-less and gorgeous, it makes me wonder why I can't look like that. But then I try to remind myself that they are most likely airbrushed and that God created me the exact way He wanted me to be.

—Kayla

Some commercials make me feel insecure, but I know that there's a lot of editing that goes on and that those girls don't really look like that. I like what the Bare Escentu-als commercial says: "Pretty is what you are. Beauty is what you do with it."

—Olivia

I'M PROBABLY THE ONLY GIRL OUT THERE LIKE THIS, BUT THE MEDIA MAKES ME FEEL BETTER ABOUT MYSELF BECAUSE THE IMAGES SEEM SO FAKE.

—ABBY

Interview with Kylie Bisutti

Meet Kylie Bisutti.

Her dream was to become a Victoria's Secret model—and she did. But find out why she walked away—and what goes on behind the scenes of many photo shoots.

Q: Why did you decide to walk away from modeling lingerie?

Kylie: The Lord opened my heart to the fact that I was not honoring Him with my body and that I was not being a real role model to younger girls. I was the girl who caused men to stumble into lust or think that happiness involves being with a lingerie model. I was also part of the illusion created by the media that puts pressure on girls to think they have to look like a model to feel beautiful or valued, when in reality I was extremely insecure myself!

Q: What are some things people would never believe happen to make models look perfect?

Kylie: You'd be amazed at all that happens behind the scenes!

1. Photoshop: Even if a model has six-pack abs and not an ounce of fat on her thighs, she will still get something about her Photoshopped—whether it's cutting her waist to get that "perfect" hourglass shape or making her C cup into a DD or rounding out her butt. With Photoshop, her lips can get bigger or her nose can get smaller.
2. Fake hair: There are always hair extensions in models' hair to give their hair more volume or length. A model's hair can be shoulder length, and on the runway it can be transformed into thick hair down to her butt.
3. Airbrushing: Models get spray tans and airbrushing to hide pale skin, cellulite, scars, and acne.
4. Makeup: Stylists can make someone look like a totally different person with makeup. From blush to eyeliner and fake eyelashes, you'd be shocked at the transformations.
5. Clothes tricks: A model may have padded underwear to make her butt look bigger or a push-up bra to add a cup size. There's also a lot of pinning that happens to make an outfit look great for the picture. That's why the same outfit wouldn't look the same on you as it does on a model.

Q: What do you think is the biggest misconception we have about models?

Kylie: It really isn't a dream job, and models aren't perfectly beautiful. Many people in this business have eating disorders to make them thin, lots of makeup to make them pretty, and spray tans to make them bronzed. It really isn't a glamorous life. There are a lot of fake things involved, and the majority of models are very insecure.

Q: What advice/tips do you have for teen girls?

Kylie: What you see in the media is all fake! You do not have to live up to this standard—models can't even live up to it. You need to stop putting all your worth and value in your outer appearance and start putting it in Christ and the beauty of your heart. Only then will you find your true self-worth and confidence. Your outer appearance will fade away, but true beauty—in the form of kindness, humility, and love—will never fade. Stop looking to the media and its illusions for your identity, and start looking toward Christ.

You can read more of Kylie's story in her book, *I'm No Angel: From Victoria's Secret Model to Role Model.*

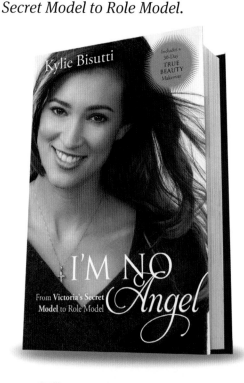

Managing Your Media

got it?

take this quiz to find out how you manage your media—or how your media manages you!

Circle the answer that best describes your response.

1. When you see a pretty actress, your first thought is

a. *I hate her!*

b. *She has a pretty face, but I bet she's dumb as rocks.*

c. *I really like the way her stylist did her hair. I might have to try that style myself.*

2. When you read a love story or watch a romantic movie, you

a. start planning your wedding and dreaming about how perfect your life will be when you meet Mr. Right.

b. think, *That's so silly—real life never works out like that.*

c. enjoy the story for what it is—a nice story.

3. When you see your favorite reality stars partying on TV, your reaction is

a. *I wish my parents would let me do that.*

b. *What idiots—I can't believe they're making such fools of themselves.*

c. *I like to have fun, but I don't have to party to do that.*

4. If you need advice about getting a dress for an upcoming school event, what do you do?

a. Go online and check out the hottest trends the celebrities are wearing.

b. Skip the event altogether so you don't have to worry about what to wear.

c. Ask your mom to take you and your friends shopping for a dress that reflects your style.

5. When you look in the mirror, how do you see yourself?

a. I get frustrated comparing myself to celebrities and feeling like I don't measure up.

b. I try to avoid the mirror at all costs.

c. I see myself as imperfectly perfect—I may not be a model, but I believe God has made me beautiful as I am.

Mostly *a*'s: Watch out, girl. You seem to think the media's images are the ideal to shoot for. Don't forget that the media uses Photoshop, fictional stories, and skewed values to make things look different than they really are. Instead of focusing on those women on screen, get to know who you are and who God designed you to be. Then live your life to the fullest.

Mostly *b*'s: While you don't believe everything you see on TV or in the movies, you tend to be a bit negative about situations. Make sure you're happy with yourself and the way God created you. Then you'll be able to enjoy the life God has given you.

Mostly *c*'s: Congratulations, my friend. You seem to handle the media and its hype quite well. You can take the good parts of the media but not let it control you. You're managing that tricky balance of being part of this world but not buying in to the hype—keep it up!

Bible Girls

The Daughters of Zelophehad:
WILLING TO TAKE A STAND

Read Numbers 27:1-8.

OUR STATUS: The five of us were sisters. Our names were Mahlah, Noah, Hoglah, Milcah, and Tirzah. We lived during a time when girls had very few rights.

OUR STORY: Back in our day, women weren't able to do things like hold down jobs or own land. Those privileges were usually reserved for men.
When our dad died, he didn't have any sons to inherit his property. So instead of standing by and watching someone else get his property, we got together and fought for things to change. We went straight to our leader, Moses, and asked him to give us our father's land.

OUR BIG BREAK: Moses asked the Lord about our situation. Guess what happened? The Lord told Moses that we should have the land! The Lord even told Moses to make a law that daughters could have property if there were no sons in the family.

By banding together as sisters, we made a change for the better in our society. Don't let the world set your standards for you! You were created by God, and ultimately you are responsible to Him, not the culture you live in. So take a tip from us, and stand strong!

Chat about It

Gather a group of girls and discuss these questions together.

1. The daughters of Zelophehad weren't afraid to stand up to the standards of their society when it came to something they believed in. What do you think gave them the courage to do that?

2. What do you think you were created to do? (Hint: Think of things you love, things you're passionate about, things you're good at, things that make you happy.) How could you use your passions and skills to honor God?

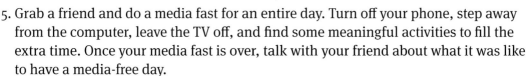

3. List some of the things about you that make you unique and beautiful. (Include both inner and outer qualities.)

4. Keep a media log for a week. Write down how many hours you spend online, on the phone, on the computer, reading magazines, or watching movies or TV. Next to each entry, write how you felt afterward. Do some forms of media leave you feeling insecure or unsatisfied with your life? How can you change your media habits for better balance?

5. Grab a friend and do a media fast for an entire day. Turn off your phone, step away from the computer, leave the TV off, and find some meaningful activities to fill the extra time. Once your media fast is over, talk with your friend about what it was like to have a media-free day.

Dear Jesus,

I love you
Me

boys, boys, boys
Chapter 3

boys, boys, boys

why they sometimes make us crazy!

Q: Why do my friends all start acting different when they're around guys?

A: Let me just say right up front: many girls (and women, too) have insecurity issues that really show up when we're around the opposite sex. There's something about being around boys and men that can bring out some real issues in us. Whether you love them or they drive you crazy, guys can really mess you up.

So let's journey together to get to the bottom of our boy issues so we can move forward and create healthy relationships with the males in our lives.

As strange as guys may seem sometimes, we really do like them. Remember the boys you thought were gross a few years ago—the ones who pushed you on the playground in

third grade and made funny bodily sounds in fourth grade? The ones who told stupid jokes last year? Well, right around junior high or so, those same boys start to seem cool to us girls. And some of them may even begin to look cute.

Now instead of ignoring those boys, we want to get their attention (whether we admit it or not)! We want them to notice us—to think we're pretty and fun to be around. We start to care about what these boys think about us.

There's nothing wrong with liking boys. It's natural—part of the way God has wired us. God made us with a desire for relationships, and it's good to want strong, trusting, healthy relationships with guys. And at the right time, it will be great for you to find the right young man who may end up as your husband one day.

But there are some things we need to get straight first. The earlier you can get these lessons figured out, the better off you'll be.

Here are some golden rules to keep in mind when dealing with boys:

- **Don't change who you are for a boy!** If he thinks you're cute or smart or that you have a good personality, he'll think so without your trying. If he doesn't, he doesn't. It might hurt if he doesn't like you, but you want someone to like you for the right reasons—not for being an imitation of something you're not. Focus more on the way God sees you . . . and becoming the person He wants you to be.

- **Don't let your relationships with boys ruin your friendships.** I know that this can be tricky. What if the guy you think is cute really likes your best friend? Well, it probably isn't your friend's fault. There will be guys who like you, and there will be guys who like other girls. Make sure you stay committed to your friends and keep investing in those relationships (see Proverbs 18:24).

- **As hard as this might sound, don't let boys take over your thoughts.** You'll have to decide what's too much . . . but if you're daydreaming about a certain guy when you should be paying attention in math class or at

youth group, that's probably a good sign that things are out of whack! We girls have a way of letting our imaginations take over, so we need to be careful about our thought lives. Sometimes we need to take control of our thoughts and focus them in the right direction (check out Philippians 4:8-9).

- **Don't define yourself based on boys.** When I was growing up, girls who hung around boys a lot were called names. Girls who didn't talk to boys at all were also gossiped about. It was almost as if you couldn't win, no matter what you did! The bottom line is: be yourself. Be happy with who God made you to be.

it's complicated!

It's easy to let guys define or even change who we are. What does insecurity look like when we're around boys?

Do you go out of your way to get a guy's attentio Do you do things you wouldn't normally do (like wear certain clothes, talk in a flirty voice, or pret to be interested in things that aren't really you)?

Do you find yourself daydreaming about boys a lot? Are you constantly thinking about how a certain guy smiled at you or replaying what he said to you? Do you make up imaginary conversations with or situations about him?

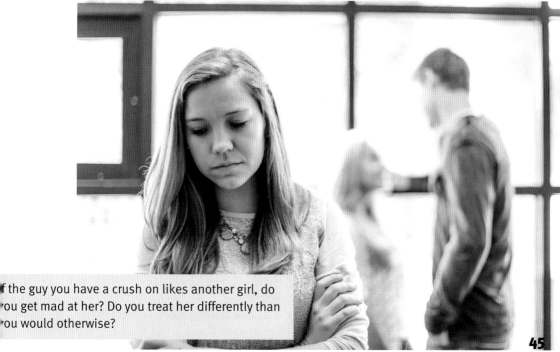

If the guy you have a crush on likes another girl, do you get mad at her? Do you treat her differently than you would otherwise?

45

want to hear about some real love— love that is unconditional and deeper than any guy could give you?

Fix your thoughts on what is true, and honorable, and right, and pure, and lovely, and admirable. Think about things that are excellent and worthy of praise. Keep putting into practice all you learned and received from me— everything you heard from me and saw me doing. Then the God of peace will be with you. Philippians 4:8-9

Give all your worries and cares to God, for he cares about you.
1 Peter 5:7

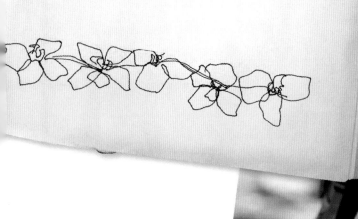

I am convinced that nothing can ever separate us from God's love. Neither death nor life, neither angels nor demons, neither our fears for today nor our worries about tomorrow—not even the powers of hell can separate us from God's love. Romans 8:38

God loved the world so much that he gave his one and only Son, so that everyone who believes in him will not perish but have eternal life. John 3:16

Your Stats

do guys

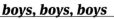

. . . the way you dress?

NOT AT ALL	SOMETIMES	A LOT OF THE TIME
20%	**49%**	**31%**

. . . how you act in class?

NOT AT ALL	SOMETIMES	A LOT OF THE TIME
20%	**49%**	**31%**

. . . who you spend time with?

NOT AT ALL	SOMETIMES	A LOT OF THE TIME
52%	**36%**	**12%**

influence. . . .

. . . your food choices?

NOT AT ALL	SOMETIMES	A LOT OF THE TIME
62%	**30%**	**8%**

. . . your interests and activities?

NOT AT ALL	SOMETIMES	A LOT OF THE TIME
44%	**38%**	**18%**

Interviews with Real Girls

how do you focus on school, God, friends, and other aspects of your life when you have a crush on a boy

Boys really aren't on the top of the list for me. When I have a crush, I don't think about him all the time!

—Taylor

If a guy isn't supportive the things I need to focu on, I won't like him ver long. That makes it easi to keep my priorities.

—Brianna

I TEND TO LOSE FOCUS ON SCHOOL MOMENTARILY, BUT THEN I REMIND MYSELF THAT I'M ONLY IN HIGH SCHOOL AND NEED TO FOCUS ON THE THINGS THAT WILL LAST FOREVER.

—MEGAN

I try to make sure that the boy has the same priorities that I do so he can encourage my schoolwork, my relationship with God, and my relationships with my friends. I want to be with someone who respects my priorities.

—Jasmine

I pray about it and try to remember that the boy isn't everything.

—Emma

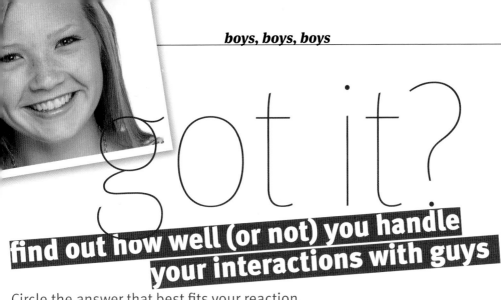

got it?

find out how well (or not) you handle your interactions with guys

Circle the answer that best fits your reaction.

1. When a boy you like is in your class, you

a. say hello to him at the beginning of class, then review your homework before class like you usually do. This is your favorite class, and you want to be prepared.

b. sit in the back and hope he never sees you.

c. pray your teacher will call on you twenty times so he will notice you.

2. You think the new guy in school is cute. You heard he goes to your church, so you

a. introduce yourself at lunch and tell him to let you know if he has any questions about the school.

b. try to avoid him, since it might be awkward.

c. give him your phone number at the first possible opportunity. You want him to be able to get in touch with you if he needs anything.

3. While hanging out at the pool, you and your friends notice several guys you don't know. They seem cool, so you

a. do what you always do—exchange magazines with your friends, take a dip in the pool, and plan your next summer outing.

b. put your magazine over your face, hoping you don't accidentally make eye contact.

c. jump in the pool, make a big splash, and swim nonstop laps. How else will those guys know that you're practically an Olympic swimmer?

4. You overhear some guys making mean jokes about the girls' basket-ball team. You were planning to try out for the team, so you

a. ignore their comments. Gossip never stopped you from being yourself.

b. don't say anything to the guys, but you start asking around to find out if other people have the same opinion about the team. You need to figure out whether you should still try out.

c. skip tryouts. You don't want to take the risk that they'd make fun of you!

5. **Your parents have a rule that you can't talk to boys on the phone unless you get your parents' permission. How do you respond?**

a. Do what they ask. You may not always understand them, but you know they want what's best for you.

b. You'd never want to talk to a guy on the phone anyway, so it's not an issue.

c. Use your best friend's phone to call the guy you like. Your parents didn't say you couldn't use your friend's phone.

Mostly a's: You seem to have a balanced perspective about guys. You don't change who you are or what you do to get their attention. Good job!

Mostly b's: While it's not a good idea to fall all over guys, it's also not healthy to hide out from them. Work at being yourself no matter who is around.

Mostly c's: Whoa. Slow down. You don't have to go out of your way to get guys' attention. It's much better to get noticed for who you are than to force it.

Bible Girls

Rachel and Leah: TWO SISTERS AND THEIR MAN

Read Genesis 29:14–30:24.

OUR STATUS: Leah was the older sister. Rachel was the younger sister—and the prettier one.

OUR STORY: Our dad made Jacob marry both of us. Actually, it would be more accurate to say he tricked Jacob into thinking he was marrying Rachel (the one Jacob really wanted). But when the wedding was over, Jacob found out he was married to Leah! Dad ended up letting Jacob marry Rachel, too, but things were never the same between us sisters.

LEAH'S PROBLEM: I don't think Jacob ever loved me. He always wanted my sister. Somehow I thought that having lots of children for Jacob would make me his favorite, but it didn't turn out that way. I learned the hard way that getting pregnant doesn't make a man love you.

RACHEL'S PROBLEM: I hated the fact that my sister had so many children for Jacob and I wasn't able to have any. I felt left out—I wanted children too. It turned into a competition between us, and I even got my servant to have children for Jacob. I ended up being able to have children of my own after all, but ultimately it felt like both Leah and I lost.

OUR ISSUE: Both of us were very desperate women. In our attempts to get Jacob's attention and fight for his love, we made a lot of painful mistakes. God used us in spite of our bad decisions, and our sons became the twelve tribes of Israel (Jacob's new name). But our family was torn apart for many years as a result of the tension between us.

Chat about It

Gather a group of girls and discuss these questions together.

1. Why do you think Leah and Rachel made such desperate decisions? What can you learn from their story?

2. Have you ever done something desperate to get a guy's attention? What happened? How would you handle things differently in the future?

3. Have you ever had a friendship that was negatively affected by a guy? How could the situation have had a happier ending?

4. Read Philippians 4:8-9. List some things you can think about that fit with each of the following words:

   true

   honorable

   right

   pure

   lovely

   admirable

   excellent

   worthy of praise

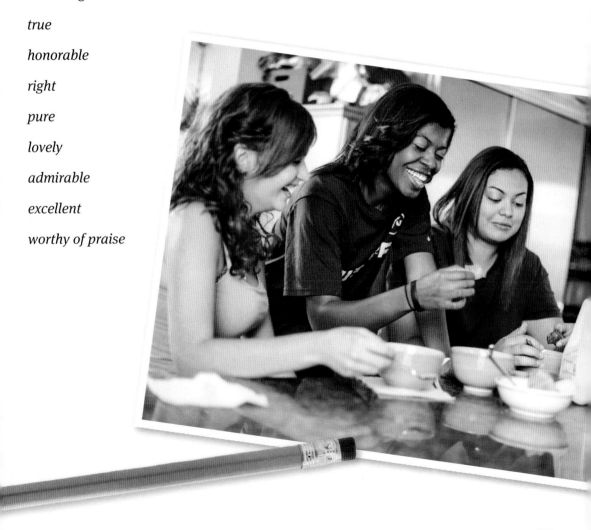

Dear Jesus,

I love you!
Me

54

popularity
Chapter 4

wanting to be the "it" girl

Q: There are some girls who seem to have it all—beauty, popularity, brains, talent, money. If I just had those things, I'd be more secure, right?

A: You know, insecurity is a funny thing. We have this idea that if we just had that one thing, we'd be happy. And we'd feel good about ourselves. From my experience, that's one of the biggest lies about insecurity—that the "it" girl isn't insecure. After all, she has that one thing that will make her happy. But it doesn't quite work that way.

If you're wondering what that one thing is, it's anything you feel is lacking in your life that would make you secure if only you had it. Let's take a look at a few of those things— the things we think will make us happy or complete or valuable. I call these false assumptions—the things you assume will make you secure but only end up disappointing you.

some false assumptions:

POPULARITY (the "it" girl = the one everyone wants to be with)
MONEY (the "it" girl = the one who has everything)
BRAINS (the "it" girl = the one who gets good grades all the time)
TALENT (the "it" girl = the one who's good at everything)
BEAUTY (the "it" girl = the one with the great hair, face, smile, and body)

It may be hard to believe, but the "it" girl is usually not as secure as she seems. The popular girl has to work really hard to stay that way. She may be so worried about what others think of her that she doesn't say what she really thinks. She may put up a front—smiling when she wants to cry, laughing things off when she's hurting inside. She may seem to have a lot of friends, but she might not know who her real friends are.

The rich girl probably wants something that money can't buy. She knows that money won't bring her true friends, and it can never replace love. She probably wishes she could have people around her who love her unconditionally, with no strings attached.

The smart girl might put so much pressure on herself to keep up her reputation as an honor roll student that she can't enjoy her accomplishments. She might be burying herself behind books because she doesn't have friends—or because she's afraid people will reject her if they get to know her.

The talented girl might be trying desperately to prove her worth through success in sports or music or other activities. As she spends all her time and energy striving for the next victory, she may not be able to appreciate the person God made her to be.

And the pretty girl—in most cases, she doesn't think she's as pretty as everyone else does. You'd never know from talking to her, but she doesn't see

"perfect" when she looks in the mirror. And on the inside, she's always wondering if people appreciate her for who she is or simply for what she looks like.

I'm not trying to make the "it" girls look bad. I'm just trying to show those of us who don't feel like "it" girls that these are all false assumptions. Even if we got "it"—whatever that one thing is for each of us—it wouldn't make us any happier or more secure. Great hair won't make you feel better on the inside. Being invited to a party every weekend won't mean you're never lonely. Good grades won't make you any more worthy. Money won't bring you happiness. You have to figure out this security thing from the main source.

That's right: you have to get your security from God.

It's time to learn what God thinks of you. Repeat God's words to yourself, over and over. Know that you're special—not because you have "it," but because you are a child of God.

what are you chasing after?

A word to the wise: nothing on the outside can ever fill a longing on the inside.

Don't forget: who you are is more important than what you can do.

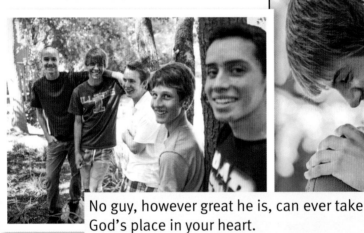

No guy, however great he is, can ever take God's place in your heart.

Some people think they'll be liked more because of their money. But think about it: Don't you want people to love you for *you*?

Outer beauty will fade away, but inner beauty makes you more gorgeous each day!

News flash: God doesn't care how popular you are. He loves you just the way you are.

if true security comes from God, then it's time to figure out what God says about us.

You made all the delicate, inner parts of my body
and knit me together in my mother's womb.
Thank you for making me so wonderfully complex!
Your workmanship is marvelous—how well I know it.
You watched me as I was being formed in utter seclusion,
as I was woven together in the dark of the womb.
You saw me before I was born.
Every day of my life was recorded in your book.
Every moment was laid out
before a single day had passed.
How precious are your thoughts about me, O God.
They cannot be numbered!
I can't even count them;
they outnumber the grains of sand!
And when I wake up,
you are still with me!
Psalm 139:13-18

You are precious to me.
You are honored, and I
love you. Isaiah 43:4

When I look at the night sky and see the work of your fingers—

the moon and the stars you set in place—

what are mere mortals that you should think about them,

human beings that you should care for them?

Yet you made them only a little lower than God and crowned them with glory and honor.

Psalm 8:3-5

YOU ARE A HOLY PEOPLE, WHO BELONG TO THE LORD YOUR GOD. OF ALL THE PEOPLE ON EARTH, THE LORD YOUR GOD HAS CHOSEN YOU TO BE HIS OWN SPECIAL TREASURE. DEUTERONOMY 7:6

Your Stats

Being more attractive: **42**%

Having more friends/ being more popular: **18**%

what do you think would make you feel happier or better about yourself?

Having more talent/skills: **19%**

Getting better grades/ being smarter: **15%**

Having more money: **6%**

65

Interviews with Real Girls

what's the dumbest thing you've

When I was in eighth grade, I went to a birthday party and slept over there. Some boys were texting my friends and asked to meet up somewhere (even though it was the middle of the night!). Since I wanted to be "cool" and not chicken, I went. When we were out walking, a cop pulled up to us and gave us tickets for being out past curfew. He took us to the police station and called our parents, and we had to go to court! Talk about going to great lengths to become popular. Looking back at this now, I laugh at myself because being popular is the least of my worries. Now it irrelevant how popular I was back then.

—Irina

I SPENT FORTY DOLLARS TO GET MY NAME PUT ON A WHITE T-SHIRT FOR HOMECOMING, BUT I GOT ONE SIZE TOO SMALL BECAUSE EVERYONE SAID THAT'S WHAT I SHOULD DO. AND THEN I NEVER WORE THE SHIRT AGAIN.

—MEGHAN

I used to compliment the popular girls' hair or makeup even if I didn't really like it.

—Lin

I remember feeling like, in order to fit in, I had to wear exactly what everyone else was wearing. And the style that everyone else was wearing consisted of jeans and shirts that cost a whole lot more than they were worth. One time I bought a pair of capri-length sweats that I thought were adorable. When I told my friend about them,

she said she'd gotten a pair of capri sweats that weekend too. I was so excited that my new article of clothing seemed to finally meet the popularity standard, so I proposed that we wear them on Friday together. She agreed, and I couldn't wait for Friday to come so I could feel cute and stylish, just like my friend. Well, Friday came, and we both wore the sweats. In one glance, though, I realized that my sweats were NOT the same kind of sweats hers were. I saw right away

that hers were a name brand, skintight, and much more expensive than mine. In contrast, mine were sale-priced and practical, loose and comfortable. I realized that day that I would never be able to live up to the style standards all my friends were following, so it really wasn't worth the chase. It's hard sometimes, but I've made a vow that I'm not going to cave to their overpriced brands,

because I know it won't really make me feel better about myself. That mentality—that vow to be unique—has helped me stay true to myself and stop caring about what my friends are consumed with.
—Jen

Interview with Tindell Baldwin

Meet Tindell Baldwin.

When she was in high school, all she wanted was to be popular. But her quest for popularity led her to an unexpected place.

Q: Why did you want so badly to be popular?

Tindell: The thing that drove every decision I made in high school was my desire to be part of the popular crowd. I was scared and insecure in who I was, so I tried to become part of a group that seemed to know exactly who they were. There were no limits to what I would try. I would become whoever other people asked me to be, as long as I was a part of the crowd. I drank because that's what I had to do to be popular. I smoked weed because if you wanted to be cool, you had to at least try it. I fooled around with boys because that's what the other girls did. I didn't know who I was; I just knew who I wanted to be like.

Q: Did you find the happiness you were searching for in the popular crowd?

Tindell: Loneliness seemed to follow me through the halls of my high school. Even when I became part of the popular crowd and was surrounded by people, I still felt all alone. I would drink to cure the loneliness, and I'd wind up lonelier than before. When I was sober, I was consumed with anger, hopelessness, and pain, but I couldn't show anyone that, because in terms of high school popularity, I had it all.

Finally everyone saw me as pretty, popular, and cool, and although it was supposed to be everything I'd wanted, it didn't matter. The pain was greater. The heartache and broken promises were biting reminders that the life I'd invested in was meaningless. I'd given up everything that mattered—my family, my faith, and my body—to chase after popularity.

Q: What would you say to girls who think they want to become the "it" girl?

Tindell: I started high school with my values intact, content to follow my older brothers' lead as outspoken Christians. I went to Bible studies, attended church events, and didn't say the f-word. The problem was that Christian life wasn't mine. I didn't have a faith I really believed in—just a set of rules to follow. I didn't have a relationship with the God I talked about so often. For me, God was a trend I followed until I turned fifteen, and then, like skorts, He went out of style.

It's easy to give something up if you never put your whole heart into it. I made the decision to leave God like you would sign up for new classes: I weighed the pros and the cons, and with what little I actually knew about a relationship with God, I chose to say good-bye. A week after I decided to leave God, I had my first beer. A few girls from the crowd I was desperate to be a part of invited me to have my first drink with them.

The truth is, I wasn't really looking for beer; I was looking for something to define me. If I drank beer, I was different from my brothers. If I rebelled, I became my own person instead of standing in the shadows of my well-accomplished brothers. I didn't realize it at the time, but my attempts to be different just made me ordinary in another crowd. I wanted everything I believed a life without God would offer me: cool friends, a boyfriend, and a chance to really have fun. And I got them all. I had "cool" friends who cared more about their popularity than me, a broken heart, and so much fun that I didn't remember most of it.

Looking back, it all seems very clear how I ended up trapped with no one who could save me but my King. Don't believe the lies this world tells you about what will make you happy. Please listen to your Savior's sweet voice and trust Him. Jesus is the only thing that will ever be enough.

You can read more of Tindell's story in her book, *Popular: Boys, Booze & Jesus.*

TINDELL BALDWIN

got it?

take this quiz to find out where you're trying to find your worth or security

Circle the answer that sounds most like you.

1. **You get a bad grade on a pop quiz, so you**

a. make a note to always read the assignments for this class. You know you can improve if you work at it.

b. sulk for a week and start making plans to join the military. There's no way you're going to get into college.

c. throw the quiz in the trash. With your good looks, you don't need to do well in school, anyway.

2. **Somehow you miss a stair and fall flat on your face in front of some popular students at school. What do you do?**

a. Make a joke about needing glasses and walk away. You're embarrassed, but at least there was no permanent damage.

b. Ask your parents to transfer you to another school. Your life here is over.

c. Say something rude to the students who are staring at you. What are they looking at, anyway?

3. **You wake up late for church, and your mom makes you leave with your hair wet and with no makeup on. How do you respond?**

a. You try to forget about how you look and focus on the service.

b. As soon as you get to church, you run to the bathroom and camp out there until your hair dries. There's no way you're going to let anyone see you looking like a wet dog.

c. You tell yourself that even without makeup, you still look better than the rest of the people in church.

4. **Your best friend already has the latest pair of jeans—the brand your mom is making you save your money for. You**

a. tell your friend her jeans look great and make her promise to go shopping with you after you've saved enough.

b. decide you can't possibly live without those jeans. You'll get the money you need, even if it means skipping lunch for a few weeks.

c. make fun of the brand of jeans in front of your friend. If you can't enjoy owning them, neither should she.

5. **It feels like everyone in your group has a boyfriend, but your parents say you're too young. How do you handle this?**

a. You talk to your parents about it again and try to understand where they're coming from.

b. You make up a boyfriend and tell everyone he lives out of town, which is why no one knows him.

c. You tell one of your friends that her boyfriend likes you. It doesn't matter whether it's true.

Mostly a's: You're well on your way to living a good life—you're able to enjoy what you have without feeling like there are certain things you must have to be complete. When something bad happens to you, you can handle it and keep on going. And when something good happens to other people, you can celebrate with them. Keep it up, girl!

Mostly b's: Watch out. You seem to get off kilter when you don't have "it." Don't forget that life is more than comparing yourself to others or obsessing over that one thing you feel is missing from your life. Learn to see the blessings God has already given you.

Mostly c's: You may have a problem with pretending. You try to act like things don't bother you, but really they do. It's time to take off your mask and reveal the real you. The only way to be content is to embrace the person God has made you to be.

Bible Girls

Potiphar's Wife: WHEN HAVING EVERYTHING ISN'T ENOUGH

Read Genesis 39:1-23.

MY STATUS: I was married to a very powerful man—the top security for the king of Egypt.

MY ISSUE: Although I had everything I could possibly need and more—lots of money, servants, a nice place to live, a powerful husband—I still didn't feel like I had enough. I got lonely sometimes, and I wanted attention. People looking at me from the outside probably thought I had it made, but I didn't feel that way.

THE PROBLEM: My husband chose a young man named Joseph to take care of the house and property. You could tell Joseph was a good man—he followed God and always did the right thing. But I was attracted to Joseph, and I wanted him even though I was married. The truth is, I wanted what I couldn't have. All my material possessions weren't enough to make me feel complete.

I tried to get Joseph to sleep with me, but he refused. This made me furious! How dare he turn me down? But Joseph loved God more than he craved attention from someone like me. He told me that my husband had been good to him, so how could he betray his master like that? Joseph knew adultery was a sin, so he ran away.

My story would be bad enough already, but I made it even worse. I grabbed Joseph's coat as he was leaving and claimed he'd tried to rape me. My husband got angry and put Joseph in jail. As a result of my insecurity, an innocent man got punished. My life is proof that money, power, beauty, and a rich man at your side aren't enough to make you happy or secure.

Chat about It

Gather a group of girls and discuss these questions together.

1. What was the "one thing" that Potiphar's wife thought would make her happy or more secure?

2. What is your "one thing"?

3. What unwise things have you or someone you know done because of insecurity? What need were you trying to fill?

4. What are some words that come to mind when you think about yourself?

5. Read Psalm 139:13-18 and Deuteronomy 7:6 and list the words that describe how God feels about you. How does this list compare to your own list of words?

Dear Jesus,

I love you!
Me

tough stuff
Chapter 5

Q & A with Beth

when circumstances hold you
hostage

Q: When I'm facing hard things in my life, I find myself getting afraid or angry. How can I handle those situations better?

A: Life can be hard—really hard. It can also be beautiful. But if we don't learn to cope with the hard parts, we will miss out on the beauty. And we'll be left with a pile of poisonous emotions from those experiences, which can wear away at our sense of security day by day. That's not the full, abundant life God intended for us.

Sometimes difficult things happen to us that are beyond our control. It's not always because we are doing the wrong thing or because there's something wrong with us. Yes, there are consequences for our sin. But sometimes we get hurt by other people's actions—whether on purpose or not. And sometimes bad things happen simply as part of living in a broken world.

Let's dig into how the tough stuff of life can cause insecurity—and what we can do about it.

Going through Significant Changes

Whether we like it or not, we all experience changes at some point. These changes may be smaller, like going to a new school or getting new teachers. But some of these changes hit you hard, like moving to a new place, having a sibling go to college, having friendships fall apart, having your mom or dad lose a job, or getting a new stepparent.

When I was fifteen, my family moved from a small town in Arkansas to Houston, Texas, the biggest city in the South. I went from a high school of nine hundred students to one with more than five thousand students. Talk about change. I had to make new friends, figure out a new school, and get used to a huge city. Don't underestimate how changes like these can affect you. It's times like these we need to hold on to God, our Rock, who never changes (see Psalm 18:31).

Feeling like You're on Shaky Ground

When your life at home is unsteady, it's easy to feel unsafe and insecure. Maybe a relationship with someone who meant a lot to you has ended, and you feel rejected. Maybe your parents split up, and you feel abandoned by one of them. Or maybe someone in your family is struggling with alcoholism, a disability, mental illness, or financial problems. Those things make a huge impact on you, especially if you feel like you have to help take care of your parents or your siblings.

These circumstances can make you feel like you can't trust anyone—like there's no one you can count on. It's normal to feel that way. But thankfully, even when everything is shaking around us, God keeps us on solid ground (Psalm 16:8).

Experiencing Death and Loss

The death of a loved one can make you feel angry, sad, lonely, or even guilty. It may take a long time to grieve and work through your emotions when you lose someone you love, and you may struggle with doubts about why God allowed it to happen.

God can handle all your feelings, but you need to be intentional about dealing with them so you can heal and keep moving forward in your life. If your feelings stay bottled up inside you, you may be left fearful about the future and insecure about life.

Experiencing Abuse

Let me make something clear here: abuse is never your fault. If you are being abused—by anyone—you are not to blame. Abuse can make you feel lonely, dirty, rejected, and ashamed, even though you've done nothing wrong. All those feelings can lead to insecurity.

Please, I pray, if you find yourself in this situation or know someone who is, talk to an adult you trust immediately. Explain what's going on and ask for help. Keep asking until you find someone who can help. Don't stop trusting all adults just because one is hurting you. There are really kind and loving people out there

who want to help you. And know that it breaks God's heart to see you going through this awful experience. Trust that He can—and will—help you when you cry out to Him for protection.

When you feel alone or scared or vulnerable, rest assured that God is with you in the midst of your pain. So what can you do when you experience the tough stuff of life so it doesn't leave you feeling insecure?

1. Read God's Word and get to know His promises in the Bible.
2. Pray to God and ask Him to help you through your tough times.
3. Talk to godly people you trust and ask for their help.
4. Keep a journal of how God answers your prayers.
5. Share your story with others. This can help them see God's faithfulness in their own lives too.

when heartache hits

Whatever you're facing—loss, change, uncertainty, or other tough times—you can take comfort in knowing that you're not alone.

One day God will wipe away all your tears.

God will never leave you—He'll be with you every step.

God sees you, and He cares about every detail of your life.

Sweet Notes

when you are going through a difficult situation, God's Word can remind you that He is there with you.

(fill in your name in the blanks)

Now, O (_____), listen to the LORD who

created you.

O (_____), the one who formed you

says,

"Do not be afraid, for I have ransomed you.

I have called you by name; you are mine.

When you go through deep waters, I will be with you.

When you go through rivers of difficulty;

you will not drown.

When you walk through the fire of oppression,

you will not be burned up;

the flames will not consume you.

For I am the LORD, your God,

the Holy One of Israel, your Savior."

Isaiah 43:1-3

This is my command—be strong and courageous!
Do not be afraid or discouraged. For the
LORD your God is with you wherever you go.
Joshua 1:9

I have told you all this so that you may have peace in me. Here on earth you will have many trials and sorrows. But take heart, because I have overcome the world.

John 16:33

DEAR BROTHERS AND SISTERS, WHEN TROUBLES COME YOUR WAY, CONSIDER IT AN OPPORTUNITY FOR GREAT JOY. FOR YOU KNOW THAT WHEN YOUR FAITH IS TESTED, YOUR ENDURANCE HAS A CHANCE TO GROW. SO LET IT GROW, FOR WHEN YOUR ENDURANCE IS FULLY DEVELOPED, YOU WILL BE PERFECT AND COMPLETE, NEEDING NOTHING.

JAMES 1:2-4

always hope

what's the toughest thing you've had to deal with in your life?

The death of a loved one: 31%
Loss of a friendship: 22%
Other: 16%
Financial stress: 12%
Not knowing a parent/not having a relationship with a parent: 6
Abuse/bullying: 6%
Parents' divorce: 4%
Illness: 3%

share your testimony.
how did God help you overcome a difficult time in your life?

When I was five, my parents got divorced. It was a very hard time for me, but I feel that God helped me get through it. He gave me strength and hope, and along the way He brought

amazing people into my life. I don't know where I would be today without them.
—Victoria

In seventh grade I suffered from depression, and it continued until I was a sophomore in high school. What brought me out of it was when my friend told me to come to her youth

conference, and there I learned to handle my depression through God's Word.
—Elisa

WHEN MY OLDER BROTHER FELL INTO ADDICTION, IT TOOK GOD FOR ME TO BE ABLE TO TRUST ANYONE AGAIN.
—ALEXIS

God has given me peace with the medical things going on with my mom. He reminded me that even if He were to bring her home, He would have her with Him.
—Jennifer

I had no friends because I had put everything into my boyfriend, who was unfaithful. I had no one else. I found a friend in God, and He pulled me out of my rough state.
—Kiara

In seventh grade my best friend betrayed me for the popular girls. They would make fun of me and spread rumors about me. Thankfully I found a great devotional that really helped me. That year I was totally changed by God for the better, and I haven't been the same since.
—Samantha

I used to have a lot of anxiety, but God has helped me overcome it.
—Maria

I was the main victim of a bully in my school, and God showed me how, even if the outcome isn't exactly what I thought, He will make it all work out.
—Jessica

got it?

how well do you handle tough situations?

Choose the answer that most closely fits your response.

1. **Your dad has been diagnosed with a serious illness. How do you respond?**

a. You stop inviting your friends over to your house. You don't want anyone to find out your dad is sick.

b. You ask your true friends to pray for you and your family. It's a hard time for your family, but you know somehow God will help you get through this.

c. You get angry when your mom asks you to help out more with things around the house. It's not your fault that your dad is sick!

2. **Your family has to move from your hometown and all your friends to another city where you know no one. How do you respond?**

a. You tell your friends you don't want a going-away party. If you don't acknowledge that this move is happening, maybe it won't be so bad.

b. You think of the move as a chance to explore a new place and make new friends.

c. You stop speaking to your parents. Even if they move, you don't have to like it.

3. **A girl at your church has told you that her mother has a problem with drinking. What do you do?**

a. You make a note to stay away from that girl. Her family has issues.

b. You talk to your parents about inviting the girl to spend the weekend at your house. She could probably use a good friend.

c. You tell your friends about the situation. You always thought something wasn't right with that girl.

4. **You don't fit in with the "in" crowd at school. In fact, you don't have many friends at all. So you**

a. pretend it doesn't bother you. Who needs them, anyway?

b. join a club or a sport at school. Maybe you'll learn something and meet a friend.

c. start vicious rumors about some of the popular kids. That should teach them a lesson!

5. **Your parents are going through a divorce. How do you react?**

a. You side with whichever parent will let you have your way and buy you lots of stuff.

b. You pray for your family and try to tell your mom and dad how you feel about things.

c. You slam your door and lock yourself in your bedroom. It will serve them right if you stay there until you're eighteen.

Mostly *a*'s: You sometimes avoid dealing with tough stuff. This can be a dangerous pattern in the long run. Even if you pretend something doesn't bother you, the emotional effects will eventually catch up with you, and you will become angry and bitter. It's time to start being honest about what you're feeling.

Mostly *b*'s: Girl, you handle the tough things in life quite well. Keep facing those difficult situations head-on, and keep trusting in God through it all. He will give you the grace you need to handle whatever comes your way.

Mostly *c*'s: You seem to get angry about tough stuff. This makes you stop talking to your friends and family or simply write them off. You have a tendency to make every tough situation all about you, even when it isn't. It's time to get a handle on your emotions and make sure they don't poison other people.

Bible Girl

Hagar : WHEN YOU GET TO THE END OF YOUR ROPE

Read Genesis 16:1-16; 21:1-21.

MY STATUS: I was the maid to Sarah, Abraham's wife. Abraham is known as the father of all God's people.

PROBLEM #1: When Sarah couldn't have a child, she got desperate. She wanted a child so badly that she made me sleep with her husband. But when I got pregnant with Abraham's child, Sarah got mad and started to mistreat me. It's true that I had been mean to Sarah first, but I couldn't stand being mistreated anymore. So I ran away. I had nothing. I was about to have a child, and I felt all alone. But even in the midst of all this tough stuff, God was still with me. He sent an angel to tell me that God would take care of me and my unborn child.

PROBLEM #2: I went back to Sarah, as the angel had told me to do, and soon my son, Ishmael, was born. But once Sarah had a child of her own, she got jealous of Ishmael. Sarah told Abraham to send Ishmael and me away. I couldn't believe it.

And so before we knew it, my son and I were in a foreign land with no food, no water, and no one to help us. I was sad, lonely, and angry. I thought we were going to die. I couldn't stand to watch my son die, so I put him down and walked away.

That's when God spoke to me through an angel again. "Do not be afraid," he said. God promised that my son would grow up and be great. He would be the father of a nation.

Right after the angel left, I got up, and to my surprise, I saw a well of water! The Lord had heard our cry.

Chat about It

Gather a group of girls and discuss these questions together.

1. What do you think was the hardest thing Hagar had to face? What can we learn about God's character from her story?

2. Share about a time when God helped you handle something difficult in the past. What did you learn about God through that situation?

3. Tell about something difficult you're facing now. How could your relationship with God help you through this?

4. What verses in the Bible have helped you deal with tough times? Write down a verse, and put it on the mirror in the bathroom to remind you that God will never leave you.

Dear Jesus,

I love you!
Me

gifts and talents
Chapter 6

becoming the girl God created you to be

Q: I don't feel like I'm good at anything. Can God really use me for anything significant?

A: This question really gets at the heart of things. You see, being a secure, confident girl goes much deeper than just being nice and healthy and positive. God has given each person special gifts and abilities to serve Him. If you embrace who you are in Christ, then you'll be able to fulfill the purpose God has specifically designed you for. You'll be able to develop the skills and gifts God has given you.

Here's the thing—if you're insecure, you're not only hurting yourself. You're also depriving other people of the unique contribution only you can make to the world. Insecurity stops us from living out our God-given purpose. When you don't use your gifts and skills, others are missing out.

Let's look at an example from one of my readers. She tells a story her husband, a basketball coach, shared:

After fifteen years of coaching basketball, for the first time my husband is coaching a team of junior high girls. He has coached a lot of boys' teams and a few young coed teams, but this is our first experience with the "group mind" of teenage girls. At practice yesterday, he called them together as a group to tell them two things. In their nervousness, the girls tried to guess what he was going to tell them. One girl guessed, "We're going to lose!" Another chimed in, "You're going to tell us we suck."

My husband was baffled. None of the other teams he had ever coached had suffered from such blatant insecurity. He looked at me and laughed. "This is the difference in coaching girls, and I see how you got started!" (I suffer from the insecurity pit.) By the way, the two things he told the girls were that (1) it was okay to be aggressive and (2) they should not be afraid to shoot more.

What this reader is saying is that girls have a special type of insecurity. It's not that guys don't have insecurity. They do—it just looks different. But we're focusing on us girls right now. You see, those girls didn't have confidence in their abilities. They had the skills—they were just afraid to use them.

Isn't that how insecurity works in other areas of our lives too? It whispers in our ears that we're going to lose or we're going to fail, so why even try? But don't buy that lie! You were born to try. Even if you miss the shot, at least you tried. And maybe you can learn something to improve for the next time.

And what about those girls who hid their talents, afraid they'd be seen as show-offs? Not only were they unable to improve their own skills, but their team was also deprived of benefiting from their abilities. A confident, secure girl understands that God created her and gave her the gifts she has. She can feel confident helping her team because ultimately her abilities point back to God, not to herself.

As you read this chapter, think carefully about what gifts and skills God has given you. Have you taken time to truly develop those talents and share them with others? If not, why not? What fears are holding you back?

When you begin to realize what you were created to do, you focus less on fear and more on God's help. This is not really about you—it's about honoring God by being the best you can be and fulfilling the purpose He created you for.

gifts that are meant to be regifted

Think about what you're naturally interested in or good at. How can you develop your gifts to help others?

an athletic girl

- can be a leader on her team.
- can model teamwork and cooperation.
- can encourage her teammates to do their best.

a smart girl

- can use her brain to come up with great ideas.
- can set an example for others by working hard in school.
- can tutor other students who are struggling.

an encouraging girl

- can help those who are having a bad day.
- can be a role model by having a positive attitude.
- can boost the spirits of those around her.

an artistic girl

- can use her skills to reflect God's creativity.
- can create things that brighten our world.
- can teach others how to make things.

a kind girl

- can help other people get along.
- can brighten someone's day with her smile.
- can befriend those who are lonely.

a musical girl

- can use her talent to lead others in worship.
- can brighten someone's day through her music.
- can help others grow in their musical abilities.

a humble girl

- can use her time to serve those in need.
- can make life easier and more enjoyable for others.
- can show Christ's love through her actions.

you have been given gifts by your Creator, and it's your responsibility to develop those skills to honor God and serve people!

He has given each one of us a special gift through the generosity of Christ.

Ephesians 4:7

I AM CERTAIN THAT GOD, WHO BEGAN THE GOOD WORK WITHIN YOU, WILL CONTINUE HIS WORK UNTIL IT IS FINALLY FINISHED ON THE DAY WHEN CHRIST JESUS RETURNS.

PHILIPPIANS 1:6

When someone has been given much, much will be required in return; and when someone has been entrusted with much, even more will be required.

Luke 12:48

No one lights a lamp and then puts it under a basket. Instead, a lamp is placed on a stand, where it gives light to everyone in the house. In the same way, let your good deeds shine out for all to see, so that everyone will praise your heavenly Father.

Matthew 5:15-16

God has given each of you a gift from his great variety of spiritual gifts. Use them well to serve one another.

1 Peter 4:10

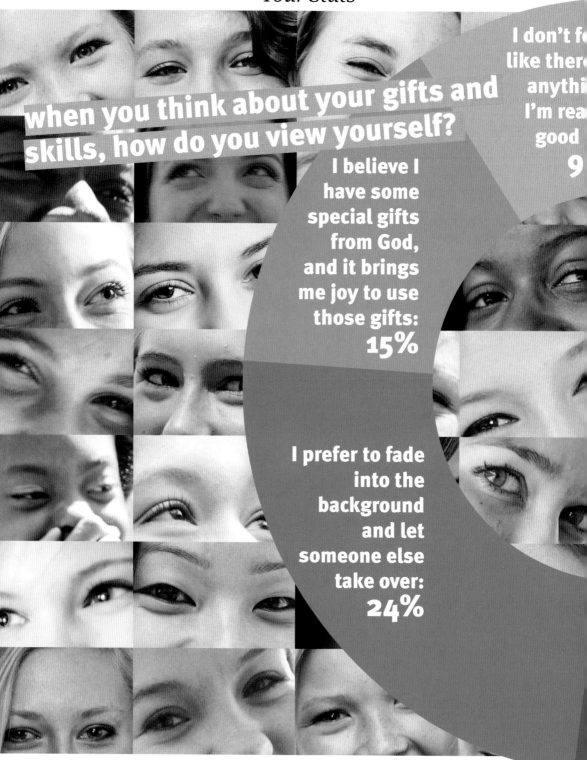

when you think about your gifts and skills, how do you view yourself?

I don't fe
like there
anythi
I'm rea
good
9

I believe I have some special gifts from God, and it brings me joy to use those gifts: **15%**

I prefer to fade into the background and let someone else take over: **24%**

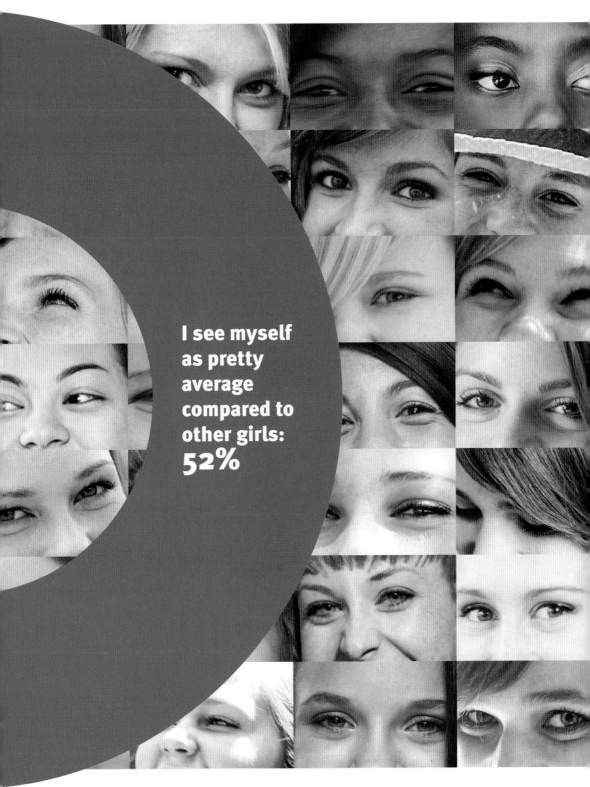

I see myself
as pretty
average
compared to
other girls:
52%

Interviews with Real Girls

what do you think your gifts are? how do you use them to honor God?

One way I use my gifts to honor God is to help with kids. I have a three-year-old sister and two younger cousins, and I give up my time to watch them and help out with them. I love them to death, and I thank God every day for this wonderful gift.   —Catherine

My gift is singing. I love using music to worship God and honor Him.

—Shanice

MY GIFT IS DANCING—SOMETHING I'VE BEEN DOING SINCE I WAS THREE. I DO A SHOW AT A NURSING HOME EVERY YEAR WITH MY STUDIO, AND I FEEL LIKE BRINGING THE PEOPLE JOY LIKE THAT HONORS GOD. I LOVE SEEING THE SMILES ON THEIR FACES!
—BRE

My gift is encouraging people.
—Genevieve

I believe God has given me talent in acting. Someday I want to be in films that spread God's light in the dark world of the media.
—Courtney

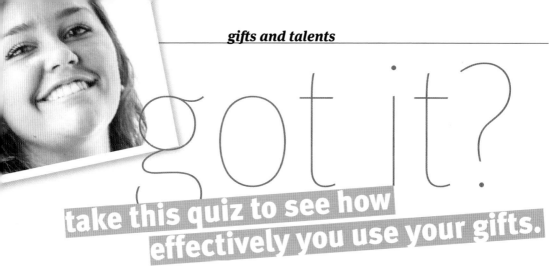

got it?

take this quiz to see how effectively you use your gifts.

Circle the answer that most accurately fits you for each question.

1. **Your track team needs two more girls to compete in the relay race. You decide to**

a. raise your hand in the middle of practice and tell your coach that you're the best choice for the relay team. You know you'd be great.

b. stay after practice one day and ask your coach to help you work on grabbing the baton. You know you need to get over your fear of dropping it!

c. start running slower in practice. That way you'll get out of having to run in another race.

2. **You're pretty good in math. You've aced all your tests so far, so you**

a. use math class to study chemistry. You figure there's nothing more for you to learn in math that you don't already know.

b. volunteer to help students in your class who are having trouble with the math problems. Maybe it will help them if they can work with one of their peers.

c. sit quietly in math class and hope no one notices that you're getting good grades. You don't want anyone to think you're a math geek.

3. **Your older sister is going to the prom and needs help choosing a dress. What do you do?**

a. You agree to help her only if she gives you credit. You want all her friends to know you were the one who picked out that fabulous dress.

b. You know what would look good on her, so you get to work finding dresses in magazines and online, giving her lots of options.

c. You'd never try to give your sister ideas about what to wear. Why would she listen to you?

4. **You've just been selected to be head cheerleader for your school's squad. But the summer practice schedule conflicts with the youth group mission trip you were planning to go on. How do you respond?**

a. You don't think twice about the conflict. You've been waiting your whole life to be head cheerleader. Go team!

b. You meet with both the leader of the mission trip and your cheerleading coach to discuss some options. Maybe you can rearrange the practice schedule or help your church with another mission project.

c. On second thought, you decide that both activities are too risky, so you opt out of both. What if something bad happened on the trip or you embarrassed yourself in front of the football players?

5. **Your teacher pulls you aside after class and tells you she thinks you should enter a national essay contest. You**

a. ask her if you'll get extra credit for doing it. You already know you're a good writer, so why waste your time if it's not for a grade?

b. thank her for recommending you and ask about the guidelines. You already have some ideas for topics that would make a good essay.

c. What? And have someone else read your writing? You tell your teacher, "No, thanks."

Mostly *a*'s: Check yourself, my friend. You may be gifted, but it's time to think through who gave you those gifts in the first place. Focus on using your abilities to help others, with the right (make that humble) attitude.

Mostly *b*'s: Way to go! You seem to have a healthy balance when it comes to your gifts. You work hard at developing your talents and using them to help others. Keep focusing on God, the giver of your gifts.

Mostly *c*'s: Remember that your gifts are designed to honor God—and you can't do that if you're hiding them! It's time to take a leap of faith, whisper a prayer, and show the world what you've got!

Bible Girls

Tabitha (aka Dorcas):

DESIGNING CLOTHES FOR CHRIST

Read Acts 9:36-42.

MY STATUS: I had two main loves: sewing clothes and helping people. I loved Christ, but I wasn't really an up-front person who liked to teach or lead. I would have rather made clothes to give to the poor.

MY STORY: I had always loved helping people and showing kindness to them. It was just something I did. When I saw that someone needed something, I stepped in and did what I could to help that person out. I especially liked to sew and make things. I guess you would call that a gift, but it was just something I enjoyed doing. And I didn't just sew for myself. I knew a lot of women who needed clothes, especially coats, so I devoted my time to making clothes for them.

MY ISSUE: One day I got very sick, and I even died. But guess what happened? Some of the people I'd helped heard that Peter, one of Jesus' disciples, was in town. They asked him to come to my house. He prayed over my dead body . . . and I was brought back to life! It was a true miracle. And sure enough, I went right back to sewing and helping people after that.

Chat about It

Gather a group of girls and discuss these questions together.

1. Tabitha's gift was more behind the scenes, but she still served Christ in a powerful way. Why do you think God gives His followers such a variety of gifts?

2. Share five things you're good at and five things that really interest you. (Some of these can be the same things, but they don't have to be.)

3. What's one thing you'd love to do but you've been afraid to try?

4. How can you use one of your gifts to honor God and to help others?

5. Ask a woman you admire how she uses her gifts to honor God. Ask her to share what gifts she sees in you.

Dear Jesus,

I love you!
Me

competition
Chapter 7

when girls get ugly

Q: Sometimes when I see other girls succeeding, it makes me feel insecure. How can I be friends with them without feeling worse about myself?

A: This is a big issue, and let me tell you—it's something women of all ages struggle with! As we talked about in the last chapter, we all have gifts. But like that cute sweater in the store, some gifts just seem to look better on other people.

As you observe the people around you, you'll notice that their gifts aren't exactly the same as yours. Maybe they have talents that are more noticeable and seem to shine brighter than yours. Or maybe you feel like they're gifted in more areas than you. Or maybe they've been working to develop their gifts longer than you have.

Wherever you go, you're going to find people who are better at something than you are. Case in point: the smart girl who knows the answer to every question, the popular girl who attracts the attention of the entire room when she walks in, the athletic girl everyone wants to pick for their team. So how do you handle it when you're around people who have gifts that are different from yours? Do you get jealous and stop being friends with them? Do you let the bitterness eat you up inside? Do you start wishing for them to mess up so you'll look better?

You've probably noticed throughout your life that things can get ugly when girls start comparing themselves to each other. And this competitive spirit isn't just evident on the field or on the court. Competition raises its ugly head in our relationships with friends and peers, too, often bringing out a mean side in people. And sure enough, it usually stems from a sense of insecurity. You might not be able to tell, but behind their mask of self-confidence, mean girls are really just secretly jealous of their victims. They are afraid they don't measure up, so they try

to make themselves feel better by finding a target to pick on.

If we're honest, there's a little bit of mean girl in all of us. A part of us feels happy when someone who seems perfect makes a mistake or reveals a flaw. Whether we like to admit it or not, that reaction stems from jealousy and insecurity. We feel threatened, thinking that if someone else is good at something, it somehow takes away from our own sense of worth. If she wins the race, I won't be seen as the best runner. If she does well on the exam, the teacher will like her better than me. If she weren't so pretty, I wouldn't look so plain.

In reality, there will always be someone better; there will always be something we don't have. But you know what? That's okay. When we can accept that, we'll be able to enjoy other people's gifts and celebrate the way God created them. We may even be able to allow their successes to inspire us to develop our own gifts—not in a competitive way, but in a healthy, encouraging way.

Make a choice today to embrace another girl's gifts. Give her a compliment. Respect her. Love her. Take note of her style, but don't feel like you need to compare yourself to her. Celebrate the good things about her while embracing your unique self.

As for the mean girls you encounter, pray for them. Cut them some slack, knowing that they're acting out of their own insecurities. And be an example to those girls by embracing who God has made you to be—and who He has made other girls to be!

friend or foe?

Sad to say, our closest friends can also be our worst enemies. Is a spirit of competition poisoning your relationships with other girls?

Heart check: Is your jealousy creeping out in the form of meanness?

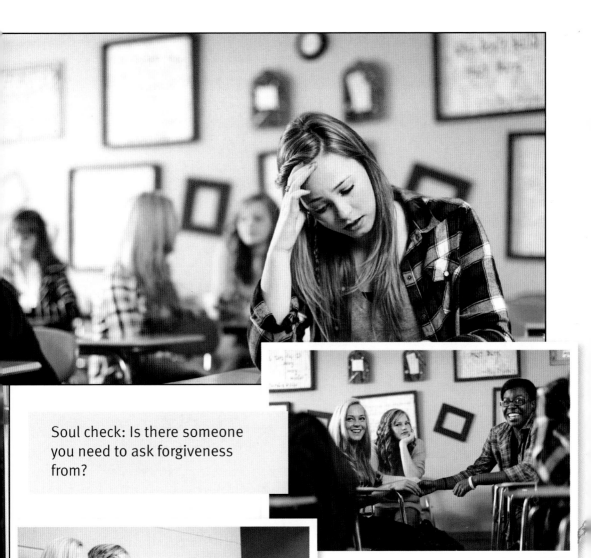

Soul check: Is there someone you need to ask forgiveness from?

did you know God has something to say about jealousy and competition? the Bible also paints a picture of what our attitudes should look like instead.

Love is patient and kind. Love is not jealous or boastful or proud.
1 Corinthians 13:4

Don't be selfish; don't try to impress others. Be humble, thinking of others as better than yourselves.
Philippians 2:3

LET US NOT BECOME
CONCEITED, OR PROVOKE
ONE ANOTHER,
OR BE JEALOUS
OF ONE ANOTHER.
GALATIANS 5:26

Let the peace that comes from Christ rule in your hearts. For as members of one body you are called to live in peace. And always be thankful.
Colossians 3:15

Get rid of all bitterness, rage, anger, harsh words, and slander, as well as all types of evil behavior. Instead, be kind to each other, tenderhearted, forgiving one another, just as God through Christ has forgiven you.
Ephesians 4:31-32

how often do you compare yourself to other girls?

All the time:
9%

Almost never:
12%

Sometimes:
31%

A lot of the time:
21%

Occasionally:
27%

how do you avoid comparing yourself to other girls?

This is something I strug-gle with. I tend to be a people pleaser and a perfectionist, and I often wish I had the qualities my friends do. I'm grate-ful to have encouraging, optimistic friends who re-mind me that I am unique

I try to think of ways that God has made me different from them. If I start feeling jealous that they have something I don't have, I try to remem-

and that my uniqueness is what makes me a strong, beautiful wom-an. I am learning the importance of surround-ing myself with people who are able to listen to me, appreciate me in a sister-in-Christ kind of way, and remind me of my strengths when I'm feeling discouraged.

ber the gifts I have that make me my own person.
—Elina

We really do become the people we spend the most time with, so I want to spend time with people who will make me feel proud of being unique!
—Jennifer

I try to find my true confidence in Christ. When I remember that, I can really look at someone else without comparison but with love instead. But of course, being human, that doesn't always

work—it's something that I have to keep going to God about.
—Ariana

I avoid comparing myself by reminding myself who I am in Christ and that He made me unique.
—Sierra

I USUALLY TRY NOT TO COMPARE MYSELF TO OTHERS. I'D RATHER SURROUND MYSELF WITH PEOPLE WHO MAKE ME HAPPY THAN PEOPLE WHO MAKE ME POPULAR.
—BROOKLYN

I try to surround myself with friends who aren't overly concerned about appearances. I also avoid television shows and pop culture things such as magazines that give false impressions. I try to make my role models be Christians instead of movie stars and singers.

—Isabel

Feeling jealous of someone? Here are a few things to try:

○ Ask yourself what about this girl is making you jealous.

○ Do you feel inadequate in this area—like you just don't measure up?

○ What can you do to improve in this area?

○ Thank God for the talents He's given you. Remember—God delights in your uniqueness!

○ Pray for this girl . . . and for yourself. Ask God to help both of you be the best you that you can be.

Feeling tempted to compare yourself to someone else? Here are a few things to try:

○ Why are you thinking about the other girl? Is it admiration or jealousy? If it's admiration, give her a compliment. Let her know you admire her and her ability.

○ You might even go out on a limb and ask the girl for a few pointers.

○ If it's jealousy, see the tips above on jealousy.

Feeling kicked around by a mean girl? Here are a few things to try:

○ Don't try to exchange jabs with her; that has trouble written all over it.

○ Don't gossip about her. Insecurity and jealousy are usually at the root of gossip.

○ Let her see your light. Make sure your actions show love, grace, and godliness. She just might need to see a real Christian.

○ Pray for her specifically every day.

And here are a few things to try . . . all the time!

○ Count your blessings, and thank God for all He's done for you. Focusing on all you have will leave little room for remembering what you don't have.

○ Pray all the time (see 1 Thessalonians 5:17). It keeps your mind focused in the right place.

○ Encourage someone. Life can be tough—you don't know what a person may be going through. Give out genuine compliments. Share a smile. Tell your friends and family how much you appreciate them.

○ Be positive. When you're looking for the good things in life, you find them. Your attitude will be better, and you'll feel better about yourself and your life.

Got it?

how do you handle competition with your friends and your peers?

Choose the answer that best fits your response.

1. **You have two best friends—one from church and one from school. For your birthday party, your mom suggests you invite both of them for a sleepover. You**

a. tell your mom you don't want a party. Then you won't have to worry about juggling friends from different worlds.

b. decide to invite only one of your friends. You're afraid that if they met at the party, they might become better friends with each other than with you.

c. go ahead and invite them both. You think the three of you will have a blast together.

2. **The new girl in the choir says she's going to sing your favorite song at the talent show. You were planning to sing it. What do you do?**

a. You drop out of the show. You're afraid she'll make you look bad.

b. You invite her over to your house to practice the song so you can see how well she sings it. If you're better than she is, you can be confident, knowing you'll show her up.

c. You keep practicing the song just as you normally would. You're sure both of you will bring your own flair to the song.

3. **The best soccer player from your rival school is moving to your school next year. You are the best player on your team now, but when she comes, things may change. What's your response?**

a. You tell your coach you won't play if the other girl joins the team.

b. You try to get the team to dislike the girl before she moves. That way even if she's good, no one will pass her the ball.

c. You get excited about having another really good player on the team. This might mean you'll have an even better team next year.

4. The kids you babysit are coming to your house today. They like your big sister better than they like you, so you

a. beg your mom to send your sister on an errand. You don't want her to be at the house when the kids come over.

b. tell the kids your sister doesn't want them to bother her today.

c. ask your sister to play a game of hide-and-seek with all of you. She's really good with kids, and it would be nice to work together as a team.

5. After lunch you notice that the prettiest girl in your class has something stuck in her teeth. What do you do?

a. You don't say anything but laugh on the inside. It's about time something like this happened!

b. You text your friends so you can all laugh about it together.

c. You quietly pull her aside and let her know. You'd want her to do the same for you.

Mostly *a*'s: It looks like you're due for a heart check! You seem to avoid situations where you feel like you might not measure up. It's time to stop keeping people at arm's length and learn to appreciate them and their gifts.

Mostly *b*'s: Jealousy seems to be lurking just below the surface of many of your relationships. You need to be careful not to let insecurity sabotage your friendships and other interactions. Learn to celebrate other people's success as well as your own!

Mostly *c*'s: Nice job! You seem to have enough self-confidence that you can recognize other people's gifts without feeling worse about yourself. Keep it up—and see if you can encourage others to do the same.

Bible Girls

Hannah: DEALING WITH THE ULTIMATE MEAN GIRL

Read 1 Samuel 1.

MY STATUS: Peninnah and I were both married to the same husband, Elkanah. But Peninnah had children and I didn't.

THE ISSUE: Peninnah was the ultimate mean girl. She was really jealous of me because Elkanah loved me more than he loved her. So what did she do? She made fun of me because I couldn't have children. It made me so upset that I cried and couldn't even eat at times. My husband told me over and over how much he loved me, but I wanted a child so much.

MY STORY: I realized I had a choice: either I could be overcome with jealousy and let Peninnah get under my skin, or I could go to God with my problem. So I went to the Lord and begged Him for a son, promising that if my prayer was answered, I'd commit him back to the Lord. And sure enough, God gave me a son! I followed through on my promise and gave my son, Samuel, back to the Lord. He became a priest and faithfully served the Lord.

I'm glad I didn't let a mean girl stop me. Take it from me: prayer will get you much further in life than jealousy ever will!

Chat about It

Gather a group of girls and discuss these questions together.

1. Both Hannah and Peninnah had reasons to be jealous of each other, but they handled the situation in different ways. How do you think their responses shaped who they were as women and how they're remembered?

2. Talk about a time you were jealous of another girl. What about this girl threatened you?

3. How do you typically handle your jealousy?

4. What can you do the next time you feel threatened by someone else's success?

5. What are some practical ways you can celebrate other girls' gifts and acknowledge your own gifts?

Dear Jesus,

I love you!
Me

secure girls
Chapter 8

Q & A with Beth

secure
girls

seeing yourself as God sees you

Q: I get that God wants me to be secure. But what does that look like in real life?

A: Oh, what a great question! I hope that after going through this book, you have a better idea of what insecurity looks like and how to handle it when it raises its ugly head. And I also hope you have a clearer picture of what it means to be secure and healthy in who God has made you to be. Let's review some of the traits of a secure girl.

a secure girl . . .

knows Christ and has a personal relationship with Him. And because of this relationship, she can look in the mirror and say, "I'm loved by God and made in His image, and He has forgiven my sins, so I have incredible value and worth in His eyes." (If you want to find out more about having a personal relationship with Christ, turn to page 150 to read more.)

a secure girl . . .

understands that her true beauty comes from the inside, not from her clothes or her outward appearance. She uses fashion to accent her beauty, not as a way to define herself or give herself worth. She has found her own style—one she feels comfortable in, not one she's using to get attention or to simply blend in.

a secure girl . . .

knows that images in the media are often distorted. She doesn't need to compare herself to models and actresses, and she doesn't think her life should be lived out like an overdramatic reality show. She recognizes that her true worth comes from knowing that God made her unique and beautiful, just as she is.

a secure girl . . .

doesn't change who she is around boys. She doesn't act different to get a guy's attention or to impress him or to avoid him. She knows that guys aren't gods or devils; they are just guys.

a secure girl . . .

doesn't base her sense of worth on being popular or having that "one thing" she thinks will make her happy. She knows that true contentment can only come from finding her identity in Christ.

a secure girl . . .

relies on God when tough things happen in her life. Those difficult situations don't shatter her; they deepen her faith and help her rely more on God.

a secure girl . . .

works hard to develop her God-given talents. She doesn't boast, but she also isn't afraid to share her gifts. After all, they are gifts from God and are meant to be used to honor Him and serve others.

a secure girl . . .

lifts up other girls instead of comparing herself to them. Instead of looking at others' gifts with envy, a secure girl cheers others on and celebrates their victories. She can thank God for someone else's gift without feeling worse about herself.

a secure girl . . .

knows she has the right to choose security. When insecurity crops up, she recognizes that through Christ, she can change her thoughts. She uses God's Word to remind her how to live. God gives her an identity and a sense of security, and nobody can take those things away from her.

the face of security

What does it look like to have real, God-given security?

there is only one way we can be truly secure as women—and that's when we find our identity and contentment in Christ.

Women who claim to be devoted to God should make themselves attractive by the good things they do.
1 Timothy 2:10

Trust in the LORD with all your heart; do not depend on your own understanding. Seek his will in all you do, and he will show you which path to take.
Proverbs 3:5-6

I pray that God, the source of hope, will fill you completely with joy and peace because you trust in him. Then you will overflow with confident hope through the power of the Holy Spirit.
Romans 15:13

I cling to you;
your strong
right hand
holds me
securely.
Psalm 63:8

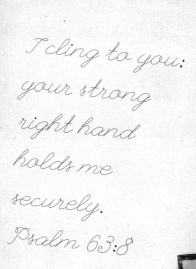

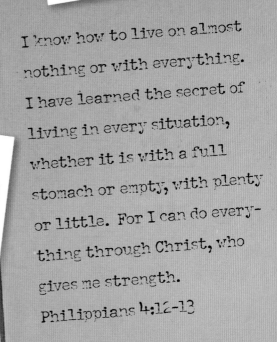

I know how to live on almost
nothing or with everything.
I have learned the secret of
living in every situation,
whether it is with a full
stomach or empty, with plenty
or little. For I can do everything through Christ, who
gives me strength.
Philippians 4:12-13

Your Stats

which of the following words do you think describe a secure girl?

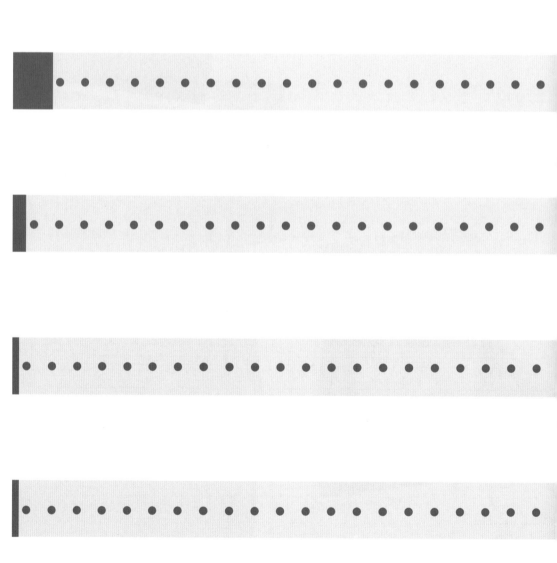

· · **Confident: 90%**

· · **Smart: 6%**

· · **Talented: 2%**

· · **Pretty: 1%**

· · **Popular: 1%**

what scriptures remind you of the truth and help you feel secure?

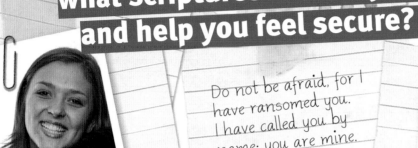

Do not be afraid, for I have ransomed you. I have called you by name; you are mine. (Isaiah 43:1)
—Elizabeth

"My grace is all you need. My power works best in weakness." So now I am glad to boast about my weaknesses, so that the power of Christ can work through me. (2 Corinthians 12:9)
—Rebecca

Don't let anyone think less of you because you are young. Be an example to all believers in what you say, in the way you live, in your love, your faith, and your purity. (1 Timothy 4:12)
—Danielle

TRUST IN THE LORD WITH ALL YOUR HEART; DO NOT DEPEND ON YOUR OWN UNDERSTANDING. SEEK HIS WILL IN ALL YOU DO, AND HE WILL SHOW YOU WHICH PATH TO TAKE. (PROVERBS 3:5-6)
--AMBER

I can do everything through Christ, who gives me strength. (philippians 4:13)
—Lauren

Always be full of joy in the Lord. I say it again--rejoice! Let everyone see that you are considerate in all you do. Remember, the Lord is coming soon. Don't worry about anything; instead, pray about everything. Tell God what you need, and thank him for all he has done. Then you will experience God's peace, which exceeds anything we can understand. His peace will guard your hearts and minds as you live in Christ Jesus. (Philippians 4:4-7)
—Emily

142

Your royal husband delights in your beauty; honor him, for he is your lord. (Psalm 45:11)
—Ashley

She is clothed with strength and dignity,
and she laughs without fear of the future.
(Proverbs 31:25)
—Aaliyah

Those who trust in the LORD will find new strength.
They will soar high on wings like eagles.
They will run and not grow weary.
They will walk and not faint.
(Isaiah 40:31)
—Nicole

Dear brothers and sisters, I plead with you to give your bodies to God because of all he has done for you. Let them be a living and holy sacrifice—the kind

"I know the plans I have for you," says the LORD. "They are plans for good and not for disaster, to give you a future and a hope." (Jeremiah 29:11)
—Brittany

he will find acceptable. This is truly the way to worship him. Don't copy the behavior and customs of this world, but let God transform you into a new person by changing the way you think. Then you will learn to know God's will for you, which is good and pleasing and perfect. (Romans 12:1-2)
—Grace

got it?

how secure are you?

Picture yourself in the following situations and decide which answer fits you best.

1. **A new girl joins your youth group. So you**

a. introduce yourself and ask her questions to get to know her.

b. wait to see how everyone else responds to her. If it looks like she'll be popular, you'll accept her as part of the group.

c. ignore her. If she needs anything, she'll probably ask.

2. **Your drama teacher announces that he'll be putting on your favorite play this season. What do you do?**

a. You find out when auditions are. You're a little nervous, but you're up for the challenge.

b. You decide you'll only be in the play if you get the lead part. Otherwise it would be a waste of your time.

c. You forget about it. You'd never do something where you could be embarrassed in front of so many people at once!

3. **Your best friend is allowed to date, but you aren't. She ends up going** out with the guy you think is so cute. How do you react?

a. You're honest with your friend about your feelings, but you also choose to be happy for her. You ask her to fill you in on things and make sure this doesn't hurt your friendship.

b. You stop hanging out with your friend immediately. She can't be your best friend if you're interested in the same guy.

c. You avoid the topic with your friend. It's not like he'd go out with you anyway, but you sure don't want to hear about it.

4. **The Sunday school program at your church needs help with the preschool class, so you**

a. volunteer to help. You like working with little kids, and it will be a good way to get involved at your church.

b. don't do anything. You'd rather do something more up front in the church so people will notice you. Why would you choose to spend an hour in a room full of whiny kids?

c. ignore the announcement. You're pretty sure the kids wouldn't like you anyway.

5. **You feel like God is prompting you to invite your friend to a youth group event, even though your friend isn't really into church stuff. What do you do?**

a. You tell your friend about the event and let her know you'd love to have her join you. Even if she says no, at least you tried.

b. You heard a bunch of girls are hanging out at someone's house that night, so you decide to go there instead of to the youth group event.

c. You ignore the prompting. You're afraid your friend would make fun of you if she found out you're one of those churchy types.

Mostly *a*'s: You're right on track. You know what it looks like to be a secure girl, so go out and keep living that way. Be comfortable with who you are, and enjoy life!

Mostly *b*'s: Well, maybe you need to re-read some parts of this book. Being secure is not about getting all the attention. In fact, that's usually a sure sign of insecurity. There's a secure girl inside you, just waiting to be uncovered. Go find her!

Mostly *c*'s: It looks like you've missed the point. Don't second-guess yourself—learn to be confident in who you are. You were created by God to be unique and special. Don't believe anyone who tells you otherwise!

Bible Girls

ARE YOU LOOKING FOR SOME

role models

IN SECURITY?

Check out the stories about these women from the Bible who learned to be secure in who God made them to be:

DEBORAH: In a time when women weren't usually seen as leaders, Deborah stepped up and led the Israelites with confidence and wisdom. (Judges 4)

RUTH: Even though she found herself far from home, in a place where she barely knew anyone, Ruth had secure, healthy relationships. (Ruth 1–4)

THE QUEEN OF SHEBA: When the queen went to visit Solomon, who had great riches and wisdom, she didn't get jealous. Instead, she recognized that those blessings were gifts from God. (1 Kings 10:1-13)

MARY THE MOTHER OF JESUS: Mary must have felt isolated and alone at times as she thought about the big responsibility God had given her, but she was secure in knowing her calling. (Luke 1:26-56)

LYDIA: When this businesswoman accepted Christ, she used her gifts and resources to serve others. (Acts 16:11-15)

PRISCILLA: As the church got started, Priscilla served in ministry alongside her husband, Aquila, teaching others about the gospel. (Acts 18)

EUNICE AND LOIS: These women were secure in their faith, and they passed on that faith to their son and grandson, Timothy, too. (2 Timothy 1:5)

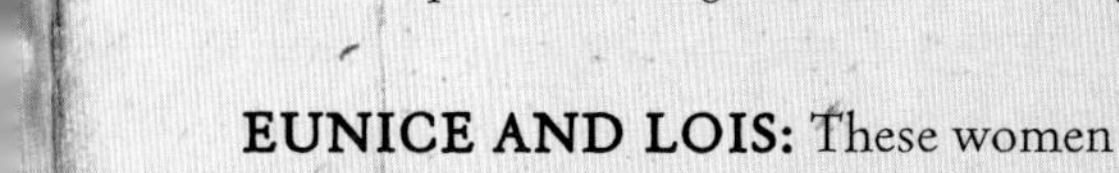

Chat about It

Now that you've read *So Long, Insecurity Teen Edition*, it's time to think about how you will live.

1. What's one thing you've learned about yourself from reading this book? What's something you've learned about God?

2. What's your biggest struggle when it comes to insecurity?

3. What one thing do you want to change in your life as a result of working through this book?

4. What one thing will you share with a friend?

5. Insecurity isn't something you're going to conquer overnight. Find a mentor or an accountability partner to keep the conversation about insecurity going.

Dear Jesus,

I love you!
Me

Prayer of Security

Congratulations! You've finished So Long, Insecurity Teen Edition, *but the road to security in Christ is a lifelong journey. Below is a guided prayer you can come back to whenever you feel especially weak or insecure and want to be reminded of the truths in God's Word. I'm praying for you on this journey too.*

My Father in heaven,
I thank You for breath this day to give You praise.
I thank You for a life where nothing is wasted,
a life where pain turns into purpose and
Your providence assigns a personal destiny.
You will never allow anything in my path
that cannot bring You glory or me
and those around me good.
No matter what this day holds,
I am clothed with strength and dignity.
I have divine strength to overcome every obstacle
and all oppression
because I belong to Jesus Christ,
and His Spirit lives within me.
You, Lord, are my security.
No one and nothing can take You from me.
You will keep my foot from being caught in a trap.
I choose to turn my back on fear because
You are right here with me.
I can smile over the days to come because Your plan for
me is good and right.
My heart is steadfast, trusting in You, Lord.
In the end, I will look in triumph on my foes.
Because of You,
I, _____, am secure.
In Jesus' triumphant name,
amen.

beginning a relationship with Christ

Maybe you've spent time in church and heard about Jesus from your family or friends, but you're not really sure what it means to have a relationship with Him. If that describes you, it would be my greatest privilege to introduce you to a saving relationship with Jesus Christ.

You may not realize it, but Christ is extending an invitation specifically to you. He has been pursuing you for years, and now if you are willing, it's time to start living the life you were created for.

It isn't hard to begin a relationship with Christ. That's because He already spent the time, energy, and unimaginable suffering on your behalf when He went to the cross. All you need to do is receive the gift He has put before you.

- accepting God's gift means you believe God sent Christ as the sacrifice for our sins.

  God loved the world so much that he gave his one and only Son, so that everyone who believes in him will not perish but have eternal life.

  —John 3:16

- accepting God's gift means you're no longer trapped by sin and instead you have the promise of eternal life.

  The wages of sin is death, but the free gift of God is eternal life through Christ Jesus our Lord.

  —Romans 6:23

- accepting God's gift means you have the promise of a full, meaningful life.

  My purpose is to give them a rich and satisfying life.

  —John 10:10

- accepting God's gift means you are made right with God.

  We are made right with God by placing our faith in Jesus Christ. And this is true for everyone who believes, no matter who we are.

  —Romans 3:22

- accepting God's gift means you have His power in you.

  I also pray that you will understand the incredible greatness of God's power for us who believe him. This is the same mighty power that raised Christ from the dead and seated him in the place of honor at God's right hand in the heavenly realms.

  —Ephesians 1:19-20

- accepting God's gift means He gives you His Spirit.

  I will ask the Father, and he will give you another Advocate, who will never leave you. He is the Holy Spirit, who leads into all truth.

  —John 14:16-17

If you want to begin a relationship with Christ or recommit your life to Him, pray the prayer on the next page.

Prayer of Accepting God's Gift

Father of heaven and earth,

thank You for sending Your Son

to die for all my sins

past, present, and future.

Today I receive Your gift of grace,

turn from my own destructive ways,

and accept Your Son as my personal Savior.

I believe with my heart

and confess with my mouth

that Jesus Christ is Lord.

Lead me daily to fulfill my destiny.

Flood me with Your Spirit.

Empower me to do the impossible.

Today the matter is settled.

I am Yours, and You are mine.

In Jesus' delivering name,

amen.

_____

Your Signature

_____

Date

If you prayed that prayer with a willing, honest heart, you have just become a child of God. You have been saved, and your eternity is secure. Words fail me to express how happy I am to point you to the Savior, who has been my joy, my strength, and my entire life purpose. Welcome to the family of God!